CHRISTOPHER COLUMBUS

The Man Who Unlocked the Secrets of the World

by
Teri Martini

Illustrated by Charles Jordan

Paulist *Press*
New York/Mahwah

Copyright © 1992 by Teri Martini

Library of Congress Cataloging-in-Publication Data

Martini, Teri.
    Christopher Columbus, the man who unlocked the secrets of the world/by Teri Martini.
        p.   cm.
    Includes bibliographical references.
    Summary: Recounts the life and exploits of Christopher Columbus, with emphasis on his faith in God.
    ISBN 0-8091-6604-6 (paper)
    1. Columbus, Christopher—Juvenile literature.
2. America—Discovery and exploration—Spanish—Juvenile literature.   3. Explorers—America—Biography—Juvenile literature.   4. Explorers—Spain—Biography—Juvenile literature. [1. Columbus, Christopher. 2. Explorers.
3. America—Discovery and exploration—Spanish.]
I. Title.
E111.M34   1992
970.01′5′092—dc20
[B]   91-44755
                                                                    CIP
                                                                     AC

Published by Paulist Press
997 Macarthur Boulevard
Mahwah, New Jersey 07430

Printed and bound in the
United States of America

Contents

Chapters   **Pages**

1. Adrift on the Green Sea of Darkness 1
2. The Secrets of the World 7
3. A Daring Plan 15
4. The Great Adventure 23
5. The Search for Gold 35
6. The Dark Voyage Home 47
7. Dreams to Give 57
8. The Haunted Settlement 65
9. A Dream Fades 75
10. The Man Who Unlocked the Secrets of the World 83
       Bibliography 86

Into the Unknown

To

Stephanie Ann Martini

1. Adrift on the Green Sea of Darkness

A white cloud passed lazily over the sun, casting a shadow on the blue-green water below. On the sea's surface a sailor nodded wearily as he clung to a long wooden oar.

His hair was soaked and matted, and his blue eyes were bloodshot from staring too long at the sun that had now disappeared from sight, leaving the air suddenly cold. The sailor shivered and made an effort to paddle harder.

How long he had been adrift, he did not know. The fury of battle still rang in his ears. Cannons and fire had destroyed his ship. Armed for defense, it was one of five merchant ships that had left the port of Genoa on the northern coast of Italy three months ago, bound for northern Europe. The ships carried a rich cargo of silks and spices from the east, and woolen cloth, copper, lead and weapons from the cities along the Mediterranean.

The twenty-five-year-old had never before sailed through the Strait of Gibraltar into the open sea. The Green Sea of Darkness, he had heard other sailors call it. On the day he left his home port, the young sailor's spirits lifted like the sails that billowed in the wind. For he dreamed of the adventures that lay ahead in foreign lands.

But as the Genoese ships rounded Cape St. Vincent on the coast of Portugal, the enemy, intent on capturing the precious cargo, was upon them. Cannons exploded and fireballs soared across the deck, killing members of the crew who did not take cover fast enough. Fire tore through the sails that only moments before were round and firm with the brisk wind that moved the ship forward.

Caught by surprise, the five merchant ships scrambled to defend themselves, but they were no match for thirteen heavily armed enemy ships. Men cried out in fear as one by one they fell. It wasn't long before the young sailor was surrounded by dead or dying members of his crew.

Dazed and wounded himself, he thought he would die too. He did not want to die, not now when the adventure of his life had just begun.

His ship listed to one side, sinking fast. There was only one chance for survival and the sailor took it. He threw himself into the sea as he had seen others do. He wasn't sure when or how he came upon the oar, but with its help he was able to keep afloat.

Hours later he was exhausted, but he dared not sleep. Then he would slip into the depths of the water, another victim of the battle. He kept himself awake by remembering the things he loved, his home and his family. Images danced in his head and he thought he could hear voices. Was that his mother calling him? Or was it the wind?

His mother's voice was soft and as gentle as her name, Susanna. She had named her son Christopher. On June 25th each year he celebrated his name day instead of a birthday, as was the custom in 1451. His name day was the feast of his patron saint, St. Christopher.

St. Christopher was a big man, a giant. He was not a Christian and his name was not Christopher at first. The giant went out into the world looking for Christ, because he had heard stories of how gentle and loving Christ was. The giant thought if he could only find this Christ, he would be happy to believe in him and do his good work. But no matter how hard the giant looked, he could not find Christ. Sadly he returned to his home beside the river.

There was no bridge near the giant's hut to help travelers cross the rough waters of the river. It was the giant's job to carry travelers across on his big shoulders. One night the giant awoke and thought he heard a child calling him.

The giant looked outside and sure enough, there was a little boy who wanted to cross the river. The giant grumbled because he would rather sleep, but he went out and lifted the child to his shoulders, thinking this would be an easy trip. But with each step the giant took, the child grew heavier and heavier. The giant was glad to put the boy down on the opposite shore.

"You are surprised that I am so heavy," the child said, looking into the giant's eyes.

"You certainly are. I might as well have been carrying the whole world on my shoulders," the giant complained.

The child's face lit up with a gentle smile. "Be happy, Christopher," he said, "for you have carried the whole world and him who made it. I am the Christ. You have found me at last. Plant your staff in the ground tonight and tomorrow you will find a living tree covered with blossoms so you may remember me."

The giant was amazed by these words. He hardly dared believe them, but he went home and planted his staff. In the morning a date palm tree grew in its place.

From that time on the giant did God's work gladly and called himself Christopher, which means Christ bearer, because this was the name the Christ child had given him.

The wounded sailor stared at the endless sea and thought of the meaning of his name. He, too, had dreamed of doing great works in God's name. He meant to be a Christ bearer, but Christopher Columbus was afraid his life was coming to an end without his having done anything. Was this God's will? Would no one rescue him? Could he possibly swim to shore, wounded as he was from the battle?

Time went by and Christopher pushed the oar before him, straining to see beyond the next wave.

"I will not die. I will not die," he chanted through cracked, parched lips. "Jesus and Mary, be with me on my way."

If he could hold on long enough, surely he could reach shore, which could not be more than a few miles away. Six at the most. Could he hang on for six miles? He wondered if he had lost much blood. Every part of his body ached and now he was hungry.

Christopher shook himself to resist self-pity. He had gone hungry before voluntarily. When he was a child, he had often stolen down to the docks in Genoa to hear the tales the sailors told of their voyages. Christopher would listen for hours, without food or drink, rather than be cooped up in his father's shop. Domenico Columbus was a wool merchant. Christopher, his mother, his brothers and his sister were all expected to work in the shop. They learned to card wool, combing out the threads to make it ready for spinning. Domenico taught Christopher to weave the threads into wool cloth on the loom.

But Christopher ached to sail the seas. Day in and day out he dreamed of exotic lands where gold and turquoise minarets topped the buildings of faraway cities, and camel caravans moved over golden deserts.

If his father sent Christopher on an errand, the boy managed to end up at the docks. He missed meals, hardly noticing he was hungry. The tall ships and the sailors' tales were food and drink enough for him.

Could he have been more than ten when he went out on a boat for the first time? The trip was short, only to a neighboring island, but the boy never forgot the roll of the sea beneath his feet. He couldn't wait to sail again, and sail he did. By the time he was twenty, Christopher Columbus was sailing regularly to nearby ports for a group of merchants in Genoa. Finally they sent him on his first long trip to a port in Asia Minor at the eastern end of the Mediterranean.

After that, Christopher knew he could never settle for a life on land. Domenico Columbus was disappointed. Two of his sons, Christopher and Bartholomew, preferred the sea to the business of making and selling wool.

When the trip to northern Europe came Christopher's way, he thought it would be the adventure of a lifetime. Now he feared the trip would be his last. He thought he could feel life leaving his body.

No! Christopher shook himself. No! He prayed for courage. "Somewhere near there is land," he told himself. "I will find it. I won't give up."

He moved more slowly now, but he moved. A wave lifted him and suddenly he caught his breath. What was that? What had he seen? Again he rose and fell back, but this time he was sure he had seen something. Sand! A shoreline! The current became stronger, a rushing tide that bore him closer to land.

A miracle, he thought. A miracle! His heart raced with joy as well as fever.

When he sighted a fishing boat, Christopher called for help. Though his voice was hoarse and he had little strength left, he made himself heard.

The men who rescued Columbus could not understand a word he said, for they spoke only Portuguese. But Christopher Columbus talked on and on in his native tongue of plans to sail to faraway places where, like St. Christopher, he would carry the message of Christ to people who had never heard it.

The fishermen carried the delirious sailor to their village of Lagos where they treated his wounds, never guessing that their act of kindness saved the man who would unlock the secrets of the world.

2. The Secrets of the World

The moment Christopher was well enough, he made his way to Lisbon, Portugal's capital city. Somehow he would have to find work because he was penniless and could not even buy food.

Red and green houses lined the crowded streets of Lisbon. Above them rose the royal palace which had a view of the Tagus River that flowed into the open sea. As he walked along, he realized he was hearing the sound of many languages. In addition to Portuguese he recognized Spanish, French, German and Arabic. To anyone who knew anything about Portugal in 1476 this was not surprising.

Prince Henry the Navigator had invited mathematicians, astronomers, navigators and historians from every country of the world to help him learn more about the earth. Though Prince Henry had died sixteen years earlier, his work continued. Lisbon was the place sailors longed to be. It was the place where daring adventures began. With the knowledge gained from all the greatest thinkers of the day, Portugal's sailors were able to take their ships south around the bulge of Africa. Her seamen ventured west into the unknown waters of the Sea of Darkness to discover islands like Madeira and Porto Santo.

Even though Columbus had long thought of Portugal as an enemy of Genoa, the joy and excitement of being in Lisbon made his head spin. He felt weak and wondered if his fever had returned. Just when he thought he could walk no longer, he heard the familiar sound of his own language. He had come upon Genoese businessmen. They took the forlorn Columbus into their homes, shared their food and helped him regain his strength.

The merchants that Columbus had been working for in Genoa had an office in Lisbon. In February of 1477, Columbus was working for them again and was sent on a business trip to Bristol, England. This time no enemy interfered with his voyage, and he sailed into the northern waters of the Sea of Darkness, which we call the North Atlantic. The young sailor kept notes about everything he saw and heard.

"At this season when I was there the sea was not frozen," Columbus wrote.

From England, Columbus visited Iceland, which was called Thule in those days, and he sailed a hundred miles beyond Iceland. Had his ship continued that journey, it would have reached Newfoundland and the coast of North America, but the constant winds that blew from the west made sailing difficult and few navigators would dare continue. The ship returned to Iceland and went on to Ireland where Columbus discovered a surprising event.

"Men of Cathay, which is toward the Orient, have come hither. We have seen many remarkable things, especially in Galway of Ireland, a man and a woman of extraordinary appearance in two boats adrift—" Columbus wrote in the margin of one of his books.

The bodies of these people were carefully examined and it was discovered that they had flat faces and high cheekbones. Everyone knew that orientals had flat faces and high cheekbones.

Columbus wondered how people from the distant Orient could reach the shores of Ireland in an open boat. Probably the people were from nearby Lapland or Finland where everyone had oriental features similar to those of the people of China or Cathay, but Columbus, who did not know this, thought he had come upon an important clue to one of the secrets of the world. China, he decided, must be much closer to the western world than most scholars thought.

Now Columbus wanted to know even more about the world. When he returned to Lisbon, he was determined to educate himself. To his delight he found his younger brother Bartholomew in Lisbon where he had started a map-making business. Christopher Columbus became Bartholomew's business partner. In those days, when it was essential to know where things were on land and on sea in order to get around without becoming lost, dependable maps and charts were important. The brothers prospered and Christopher was glad to find work that would keep him in Lisbon for a time so he could learn from the scholars he met in the city.

The printing press had recently been invented and Columbus wanted to read everything that had ever been written about the world. Night after night he pored over his books. He discovered the adventures of Marco Polo's travels to the court of Kubla Khan in China by reading Marco Polo's book. He studied the geography of Ptolemy, the brilliant Egyptian, and he read the Bible.

On Sundays Columbus went to mass in the chapel of the Convento dos Santos and thanked God for the gift of life. He never forgot how God had spared him after the battle with the Portuguese merchant ships. Columbus was convinced God had chosen him for some important work. What this great work was, he did not know. When the time came, God would reveal his plan.

As Columbus became better educated, he met new and interesting people. One Sunday at mass he met Dona Felipa Perestrello e Moniz, a young woman who went to the boarding school connected with the convent. Dona Felipa was the daughter of one of the first families of Portugal. Her father and her brother had been navigators, and now her brother was governor of the island of Porto Santo, which was one of a group of Portuguese islands that lay some 700 miles offshore in the Sea of Darkness. Dona Felipa was impressed by the tall, blue-eyed Columbus who entertained her with tales of his adventures at sea and the things he had learned in books.

In 1749, three years after coming to Portugal, Christopher Columbus married Dona Felipa. When their son Diego was born in 1480, Columbus became a merchant to support his growing family. But he could not forget the call of the sea for long.

The Portuguese were trying to reach and round the tip of Africa. With the Turks in control of the

Holy Land, and the Moors, who were also Muslems, in control of northern Africa and part of Spain, it was dangerous for Christians to travel to the Orient by way of the Mediterranean Sea and through the Holy Land to China as Marco Polo had done.

Still, the western world needed the products of the east. Spices helped preserve food and made it tasty. There were gold and rare jewels to be found in the east, as well as silk. Merchants were anxious to find a better, safer way to get the spices and gold they wanted. The Portuguese found some gold and spices along the African coast. Each year they sailed farther and farther south. Columbus longed to go with them and sail past the equator.

In 1481, the new king of Portugal sent expeditions south of the bulge of Africa where gold had been discovered. Columbus was on one of these voyages. On the journey he came across another piece of valuable information. Because of the great heat expected at the equator, it had long been suspected that people could not live in the tropics around the middle of the earth and that sailors could not survive in tropical waters.

Columbus wrote another important note to himself about the torrid zone around the equator.

"The torrid zone is not uninhabitable, for the Portuguese sail through it today and it is even very populous . . ."

To Columbus this meant the waters around the equator were not to be feared by sailors.

It was while visiting his brother-in-law on the island of Porto Santo that Columbus heard about a curious kind of driftwood that had been washed ashore on the islands. The wood was from a tree unknown on any of the nearby islands. What was most mysterious about the wood was that it had been carved, but not with iron as was the custom in Europe. Who had carved the wood and where were trees grown that produced such wood? There were also strange seeds washed ashore from plants no one recognized.

Columbus and his brother-in-law, who was also a navigator, talked about these unknown seeds and the mysterious wood. Columbus thought these clues, and all the others he had gathered, proved that the Sea of Darkness was not nearly as wide as most people thought, nor were the waters of the far north or of the south to be feared.

Columbus concluded that if a man had the courage, he could sail west and reach China, India and Cipangu, which was Marco Polo's name for the island of Japan. But what man would dare sail far enough and long enough on the Sea of Darkness to discover the truth of this notion, when finding your way on an ocean that had not been charted was so uncertain?

What if, Columbus thought, he were the man who was daring enough to make the voyage that would unlock the secrets of the world?

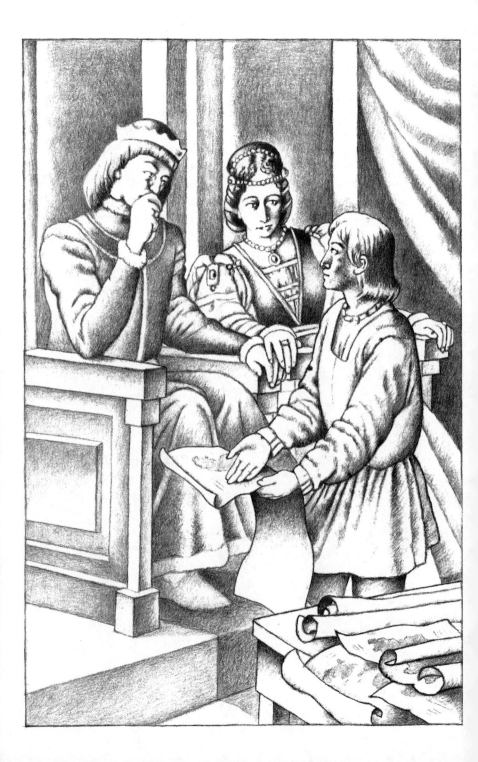

3. A Daring Plan

Christopher Columbus and his five-year-old son Diego walked along the dusty road from Palos, Spain, to the monastery of La Rabida. Their trip from Portugal had been hurried and secret because Columbus was so deeply in debt he was in danger of being arrested. He needed time and freedom to earn the money to pay his angry creditors. He also needed someone to care for little Diego, because Dona Felipa had died. The monks at La Rabida would take Diego in and educate him while Columbus straightened out his business affairs.

Now as he and Diego approached the Spanish monastery, Columbus saw his son's steps falter. Poor Diego! He was too tired to walk any more. Columbus lifted the child to his shoulder. Weary as he was, the little boy gave his father a beautiful smile that touched Columbus' heart and he felt a surge of love and new purpose.

Someday, he vowed, someday Diego would be wealthy and honored as the son of Christopher Columbus. By San Fernando, he would!

Once Diego was settled with the monks, Columbus went off to find someone with the money he needed to carry out his daring plan, which he called the Grand Enterprise. The key to this plan was the new picture Columbus had gained of the earth and the estimated distances between continents. The time it took for Columbus to come up with this picture kept him from his work and drove him into debt, but he felt that his plan was worth any risk if it succeeded.

For centuries educated men had tried to estimate the size of the world. Columbus worked with new figures which were based on his own studies. He was convinced that the world was much smaller than everyone thought—ten percent smaller. He determined that there were only 2400 miles between Spain's Canary Islands off the coast of Africa and what Marco Polo called Cipangu, or Japan, an island whose gold-roofed cities promised great wealth. Columbus felt this distance could be navigated by a man like himself who had faith that God meant him to make the voyage.

But who would respect the ideas of a poor weaver's son who had educated himself? Columbus needed the opinion of a learned man to support his calculations. He heard that Poalo Toscanelli, a much-respected physician and scholar who lived in Florence, Italy, had estimated the distance between Spain and where Cipangu might be at 3000 miles. What would Toscanelli think of an estimate of only 2400 miles? Columbus wrote to the elderly scholar and received an answer.

"To Christopher Columbus Paul the Physician sends greetings:

I observe thy great and noble ambition to pass over to where the spices grow," the letter began.

Toscanelli was so encouraging in his letter that Columbus wrote to the scholar again, explaining the reasoning behind his estimate of 2400 miles between the Canary islands and Cipangu.

If the island of Cipangu did exist, as Marco Polo said it did in his book, and if that island was farther off the coast of China in the Ocean Sea, say 1500 miles, then a calculation of the distance of 2400 miles between European territory and the Orient should be logical.

In his second letter Toscanelli agreed that by sailing west for 2400 miles, Columbus might well reach that golden island of Cipangu and from there sail to the rest of the Orient.

Columbus was delighted with this answer. Other scholars would respect Toscanelli's opinion and, therefore, respect Columbus too. Armed with Toscanelli's letters, Columbus first went to King John of Portugal and described his Grand Enterprise.

Columbus was taller than most men at the King's court and his eyes sparkled with ambition. But it was his confidence that impressed the king.

"With the help of the Holy Trinity, I can sail west to the Orient," Columbus said.

Ships, men and provisions for the long journey were all he needed. A small investment of money would make this dream come true. The king need not send his navigators in search of a long way around Africa to China when there was a direct route across the Ocean Sea. No longer should that sea be called the Green Sea of Darkness. The king had only to give Columbus what he needed and Columbus would bring the light of day to those mysterious waters and unlock the secrets of the world.

Once the first daring trip was made successfully, Portuguese ships would sail the Ocean Sea regularly, carrying treasures from Cipangu, China and the Indies. These treasures would make Portugal richer than any other country in Europe. Portuguese missionaries could join the merchant ships and carry spiritual riches of the Christian faith to the people of the Orient. King John would be blessed indeed as the monarch who saw the wisdom of Columbus' plan.

King John listened, excited by this man whose rich voice held the promise of blessings, wealth and honor. The king wanted to believe Christopher Columbus, but was all that Columbus said true? Was such a trip possible? The king had no way of knowing, so he turned the matter over to his advisors who consulted scholars.

Columbus waited a whole year for a favorable answer, but he was disappointed. The scholars were not impressed with the Grand Enterprise.

There was no reason to believe that Ptolemy was wrong about the size of the earth and that Columbus was right, the scholars said. They did not believe in the golden isle of Cipangu which Marco Polo mentioned and said himself he had never seen. The only lands on the other side of the Ocean Sea were China and India. Even Paolo Toscanelli said the distance to China was 5000 miles. Three small ships could not carry enough food for such a long journey. The sailors would starve to death before they reached land and the ships would be lost. It was a foolish plan and the king should not invest in it, they decided.

Even though Portugal had said no, Columbus was not discouraged. He believed in God and in prophecies. In the writings of a Roman scholar who had lived nearly 1500 years earlier, Columbus had read this passage which he never forgot.

"An age will come after many years when the Ocean will loose the chains of things, and a huge land lie revealed . . ."

Columbus was convinced that land was Cipangu and he was equally certain God had chosen him to discover it. He left Portugal to look for wealthy investors in Spain.

Count Medina Celi, a ship owner, was fascinated by the Grand Enterprise. He was anxious to invest in the plan, but he and Columbus agreed it was important to have the approval of a strong country like Spain or Portugal behind the Enterprise. An ordinary explorer on his own would not have any standing in a foreign country. Columbus must carry impressive papers from royalty which approved his trip and sent greetings from one royal family to another.

Columbus went to seek the aid of Spain's King Ferdinand and Queen Isabella. Queen Isabella liked the bold navigator at once, perhaps because she and Columbus were very much alike. They were both about thirty years old when they met. Both had strong personalities. Both were Catholics interested in spreading Christ's message to new lands.

But after studying the Grand Enterprise, the Spanish Advisory Committee came back with an unfavorable decision. Like King John's advisors, they could not believe the world was as small as Columbus said it was. They did not believe in Marco Polo's Cipangu or any other islands of the Indies. India and China were the only lands of the east. Columbus, they thought, was nothing but a braggart.

Even though the committee said no to the plan, Queen Isabella remained friendly. She told Columbus not to give up hope and she even helped pay his expenses while he lived in Spain. Columbus felt he had nothing to lose by waiting for King Ferdinand and Queen Isabella to change their minds. He waited six-and-a-half years. During that time Columbus continued his studies and made new friends. He met a lovely woman, Beatriz Enriques de Harana, who became the mother of his second son, Ferdinand.

Once in 1488, Columbus returned to Portugal to ask King John to consider the Grand Enterprise again. But as Columbus arrived in Lisbon, Bartholomew Dias' ships sailed into port. Dias had found the tip of Africa and gone around it. It was only a matter of time before another explorer sailed from the tip of Africa to India and China. King John now had his own water route to the Orient. He did not need Columbus.

Columbus returned to Spain while his brother Bartholomew presented the Grand Enterprise to England and France. Both countries turned him down. The waiting went on.

In 1491, the costly war Spain had been fighting against the Moors, who had invaded their country and tried to spread the Muslim religion, was suddenly over. The Moors left and Spain was a united Catholic country again.

At the suggestion of Father Juan Perez at the monastery of La Rabida where Diego was still at school, Columbus went to Queen Isabella again. Now that the country was no longer engaged in war, perhaps the king and queen would have more money available.

Columbus' hair and beard were growing gray, but his eyes were still bright and burning with the power of his dream. When Spain said no again, Columbus finally gave up.

"I will take my plan to France myself," he decided.

He set out for the nearest port. He was four miles from the royal palace at Santa Fe when a messenger from Queen Isabella caught up with him. The queen had changed her mind.

One of her advisors had told her she was foolish not to risk so small an amount of money for such great glory for God and Spain. If Columbus was right, Spain would become the richest and most powerful country in the world. Thousands of people would be converted to the Catholic faith. Count Celi was still interested in the investment and was ready to give money. If Columbus could come up with other investors on his own, the king and queen would now provide whatever else was necessary, including a passport that would let the world know the Spanish royal family was behind Christopher Columbus.

The king and queen even agreed to the high price Columbus asked for his services. He demanded ten percent of the money Spain would make from his discoveries. This income would continue throughout his lifetime and that of all his heirs. He insisted on being given the title of Admiral of the Ocean Sea, which would put him in charge of every ship and every captain that sailed that sea out of Spain. He asked for and got the title of Viceroy, or ruler, of all the lands he would discover. All these honors would be his if, and only if, his daring plan was a success.

But Columbus knew he would succeed and was glad that his Grand Enterprise was under way at last.

4. *The Great Adventure*

As a fine for smuggling, the city of Palos owed the king and queen of Spain two ships. On May 12, 1492, Columbus went to collect them. After hiring a third ship he had a little fleet made up of the Santa Maria as his flagship, the Pinta and the Nina. It took nearly three months to outfit the ships and hire their crews.

In the early hours of the morning of August 3rd, the Church of St. George in Palos was crowded with more than ninety seamen who made their communion and asked God to bless them on their voyage across the Ocean Sea. No one knew what to expect, though Captain General Christopher Columbus was confident that after a few weeks' sailing, perhaps a month, the secret of what was on the other side of the dark sea would be revealed.

If Columbus was right, every man would become rich from his share of the gold and treasures of the Indies. But if he were wrong, all three ships might be lost in unknown waters. Most of the Spanish sailors had little confidence in Columbus, who was, after all, a foreigner. The seamen were inspired to sign up for the voyage by their own Spanish captain, Martin

Alonso Pinzon, who believed in the Genoese navigator's plan.

Pinzon said this trip would be the adventure of a lifetime. It was Pinzon's enthusiasm that made the sailors overlook the fact that Columbus had never commanded a ship before, much less a fleet of three caravels. What the sailors did not know was that Christopher Columbus had taught himself to be one of the best navigators who ever lived.

After mass on that August morning, Columbus proudly boarded the Santa Maria and gave the order to set sail in the name of Jesus Christ. The Pinta, commanded by Captain Martin Alonso Pinzon, and the Nina, under Captain Vincent Yanez, followed. Each of the ships had fresh white sails painted with bold red crosses. This was a mission for God as well as one of discovery. To the islands of the Indies and China itself, the travelers would bring Christ's message.

Slowly the ships sailed down the Tinto River on the outgoing tide to the open sea where a fresh breeze filled the sails. The voyagers had made a good start. By sailing south and west they would reach Spain's Canary Islands in six to ten days. There the fleet would anchor to take on supplies and the crew could make final adjustments to the caravels. The Nina's triangular sails were already proving troublesome. Columbus felt the ship would be more seaworthy with sturdy square sails like the Pinta and the Santa Maria. In the middle of that first morning at sea Columbus went to his cabin to say his private prayers, something he did several times each day no matter where he was.

The great adventure really began on September

6, 1492, when the ships left the Canary Islands. With the known world behind them, Columbus and his men sailed where no one had sailed before. Their route was along the 28th north latitude, where Columbus expected to find winds that blew from the northeast instead of the west, something he had learned on his trip to Africa. With these trade winds blowing from behind, the ships would be steadily pushed across the sea westward.

The crew was filled with an uneasy excitement, for they were used to sailing within sight of land. But Columbus' confidence calmed the sailors. In spite of themselves the men were impressed by their strong, God-fearing leader. The first few days and nights passed without trouble.

Time on the Santa Maria was marked by a half-hour glass that was kept beside the ship's wheel. Every half hour, the glass was turned over with a little ceremony that included a prayer. The half hour was marked on a chart. Columbus estimated the ship's speed by studying the movement of bubbles or seaweed in the water. The speed, multiplied by the number of hours passed, gave the distance the ship traveled. This method of navigation is called "dead reckoning." It was the only method Columbus knew, but he knew it well.

With the use of dead reckoning to tell how far he had gone, and with a magnetic compass to show his direction, Columbus plotted his position on his maps and charts. When the fleet had gone 2400 miles, it would reach land. To spur the crew on, the king and queen of Spain had promised a prize of a great deal of money to the man who first sighted that land.

From Cipangu Columbus thought the ships could sail on to China, India and other islands of the Indies, picking up provisions and gold everywhere they stopped. He imagined visiting the courts of kings and presenting the letter of recommendation from their Royal Catholic Majesties of Spain. He dreamed of the gold-roofed cities that Marco Polo had described and of the splendor of the royal court of the Great Khan of China.

But as the days went by with no sign of land, the men grew restless and worried. They listened to the east winds that blew them westward and wondered if there would be west winds to blow them eastward on the return trip. Columbus knew the seamen might become paralyzed by their fears and insist on turning back.

On September 9th, Columbus decided to keep two records of the journey. One record would show the real distance traveled, which he would keep secret. The other record, which would show a shorter distance, he would give to his men to keep them from worrying.

Four days later on the thirteenth of September, the sailors were alarmed by a sudden change in the compass needle. It was customary for the ship's pilot to check the position of the north star with the magnetic needle of the compass. This checking was called the "pilot's blessing," because the pilot raised his arm so that his hand was between his eyes to cover his view of the north star as if in blessing. The pilot then brought his hand down on the compass point which should mark true north. On this night the pilot discovered the compass was off a full point from true north. Word spread quickly and the men were terrified.

Where were they? Couldn't they depend on the compass any longer? How could they tell where they were if the compass was off in these strange waters?

Columbus was able to calm the men.

"The north star *appeared* to move because of its position in the heavens in relation to our position on the earth. Nothing is wrong," he said.

When the "pilot's blessing" was performed a few days later, sure enough, the compass was back to normal.

On September 14th the air was cool and fresh. At sunrise the youngest boy on board the Santa Maria sang the morning prayer which might have been similar to this one.

Blessed be the light of day
and the Holy Cross, we say;
and the Lord of Veritie
and the Holy Trinity . . .

As quoted by Samuel Eliot Morison
in *Admiral of the Ocean Sea* page 172.

In the middle of each day the sailors prepared their one meal in a fire box on the deck. Chick peas and beans cooked in olive oil, some biscuits or bread, and a measure of wine were not the kinds of food the men would have liked, but meat and fresh vegetables spoiled quickly on board. Seamen had to make do with what they had.

Some time during the eighth day at sea there was a stir of excitement. Two birds blew on board. Did this mean land was near? The Santa Maria flashed a signal to the Nina and the Pinta. Sailors climbed the masts, searching the horizon for land, but none appeared. The winds continued to blow the ships in a westerly direction.

Two days later great bunches of blue seaweed appeared. Again the men were hopeful. Weeds suggested that land was nearby.

But Columbus believed the ships had not come nearly far enough to reach land. As the days went by, the seaweed became thicker and thicker. Soon the ships were surrounded by weeds as far as the eye could see. Panic spread.

"The seaweed will become so thick, our ships will be caught in it and never move again," the sailors said.

Captain Pinzon and Captain Yanez insisted on trying to find a way out of the seaweed. Time was wasted while the captains varied the course to do this. Finally Pinzon and Yanez listened to Columbus who said, "Adelante! Onward! Sail onward!"

He had read about this weed which he believed would not endanger the ship. And he was right. The expedition had sailed into the Sargasso Sea, named for the sargassum, weeds that grow on the surface of the water. He told his men the weed looked dangerous but was not. Columbus reset his westward course and sailed on.

By September 19th the voyagers had traveled

1291 miles according to Columbus' secret record. Halfway there! They had made good time. But then the wind calmed and changed to a westerly direction on September 22nd. The ships were now sailing into the wind and the fleet went slowly, only 200 miles in five days. The sea was so calm the men went swimming, something they enjoyed, but they worried that the winds would remain calm and the ships would be stranded.

"We will find the northeast winds again," Columbus said. "These west winds will bless our way home," he added, pointing out that westerly winds *did* blow in these waters.

When the winds remained calm for three days, Captain Martin Alonso Pinzon sent a chart over to Columbus on a rope from his ship. Pinzon felt they should change course and look for islands he thought must be nearby according to his chart.

Columbus was studying the charts at sunset when Pinzon, who was searching the southwestern horizon, suddenly shouted, "Land! Land, sir. The royal prize is mine!"

Sailors scrambled to climb the rigging, many saying that they, too, saw land. But at dawn there was no sign of land and everyone was disappointed. What they had seen was a false landfall, only sky and clouds. The sailors went about their work more slowly, wondering if they were crazy for coming on this journey.

For the next six days the light winds continued, but someone caught a dolphin and the fresh food cheered the weary sailors. The cheerfulness did not last because everyone knew the drinking water and food supplies were running low.

"This Genoese captain is a madman. He will kill us all!" the men complained.

Some of the ship's officers finally asked Columbus to turn back. He refused, though he knew everyone was angry and frightened enough to kill him and take over the ship.

"But think of it. If you return to Spain without me, their Royal Highnesses will surely hang you all," Columbus said. "Why give up now? Think how far you have come, too far to turn back when the riches of the Indies are only a few days away."

The wind would grow stronger, he told them. It always did and the ships would move quickly again.

On October 2nd the winds did change and suddenly the ships raced along. More birds were seen. Four days later the ships passed the spot where Columbus expected to find Cipangu. He was not concerned because he assumed the island was only a bit north or south of their present position. If they missed Cipangu on the way out, they could go to China first and visit Cipangu on the way back.

On October 10th Columbus noticed a flock of birds and changed his course to follow them, hoping the birds would lead the ships to land. The change in course made the men think Columbus had doubts about their destination. They had been sailing for thirty-one days and even the public record of their trip showed the fleet had come 3000 miles. Would any of them ever see Spain again?

Responding to the sailors' fears, Captain Martin

Alonso Pinzon came aboard the Santa Maria for a talk with the Captain General. Afterwards, Columbus announced they would sail two or three more days. If land was not sighted, he would turn back.

On the evening of October 11th, the Salve Regina was sung at 5:30 as usual. The men were far too restless afterwards to sleep. Everyone stared into the glow of the setting sun. The wind picked up and this night Columbus decided to break the rule he had made about not sailing in the dark to avoid running into rocks. If land was near, they must find it now or never. He alternated between pacing the deck and praying in his cabin.

Two hours before moonrise at 10 p.m. Columbus was peering into the darkness and had the heart-stopping experience of seeing a light.

"No more than a wax candle rising and falling," he said, "but a light."

Not wanting to raise hopes too soon, he confided in only two of his men.

"Look. Do you see it?" he asked urgently.

"I see it, sir," Pedro Guitierrez replied.

"I do not," the second man said.

"Very well," Columbus said. "Tell no one."

Four hours later, at 2 a.m. on October 12, 1492, Rodrigo de Triana on the Pinta spotted white sand shining in the moonlight.

"Tierra! Tierra!" he shouted, nearly falling from the rigging in his excitement.

The men picked up the cry, their voices rising like wind in a storm.

"Tierra! Tierra!" The sailors' red stocking caps bobbed wildly as the good news spread. Their chanting became a prayer.

Aboard the Santa Maria, Columbus' heart sang with joy and thanksgiving. God, indeed, helps those who dare all things in his name.

5. The Search for Gold

At sunrise the Santa Maria, the Nina and the Pinta sailed triumphantly through clear blue water to an island that no European had ever seen. Columbus expected to be greeted by friendly oriental people wearing rich silk and brocade clothing.

He saw no one.

A lush green forest rose above coral sands. Tropical birds with brilliantly colored plumage flew from the branches of hardwood trees and circled the small fleet. Columbus recalled what Marco Polo had written about Cipangu.

"The king of the island hath a mighty palace, all roofed with finest gold . . ."

There was no palace in sight, no buildings at all. Columbus concluded that he had not reached Cipangu after all. Instead he had come upon one of the smaller islands of the Indies. But where were the people? Was the place uninhabited?

Carefully Columbus directed his fleet's approach to the island. The caravels were soon riding at anchor in a small deserted harbor while the captains and their men rowed ashore carrying the banner of the royal expedition, a green cross on a white background. Once on land, the men fell to their knees, kissed the sand and thanked God for their safe journey. Sailors bowed to Columbus and called him Admiral with great respect, for he had earned that title with the success of his voyage.

Planting the banner and a cross, Columbus claimed the land for Queen Isabella and King Ferdinand. A religious ceremony followed and the men recited prayers and sang joyously. Then at last the people of the island came forward—and what a surprise they were!

Creeping timidly out of the woods and onto the gleaming sands, they stared in awe at the white men and their tall ships. The islanders were handsome people with dark straight hair, broad foreheads and olive-colored skin. To everyone's astonishment the Indians, as Columbus called them (for he thought he had discovered the Indies) wore nothing at all.

"They go quite naked as their mothers bore them," he wrote in his journal.

The Indians painted their bodies with red, black or white paint. Some painted the whole body, while others painted only the eyes or nose. They were friendly people, who treated the explorers with respect and affection as if they were visiting gods.

Everything about the visitors fascinated the Indians who spoke quickly, intelligently and repeated anything that was said to them. They even imitated the prayers they heard and the sign of the cross.

They were anxious to offer gifts of fruit and woven cotton, as well as darts, which appeared to be their only weapons. The darts had been cleverly made of sticks and a fish's tooth for a sharp point.

There seemed to be no animals on the island except for parrots with brilliant green feathers, which were also offered as gifts. In return Columbus gave the Indians colored beads, red caps and small hawk's bells whose soft tinkling soon filled the air. The Spanish swords created quite a stir, but the Indians did not understand what they were. When one of the men drew his weapon to show it off, an Indian grasped the metal blade in his bare hand and cut himself.

Columbus observed that some of the Indians had scars on their bodies. By using sign language, he learned that these scars came from battles with a fierce tribe to the south which invaded the island from time to time and tried to carry some of the islanders away.

Late in the afternoon, the sailors returned to their ships and the Indians followed in their own boats, some large enough to hold forty-five people, others so small they held only one man. Because the paddles were not attached, the men could dig them deeply into the water with strong strokes so that the boats moved remarkably fast.

The Indians returned to the island at nightfall, but came back the next day to trade again. They wanted anything at all; even part of a broken glass pleased them because it was something that belonged to these wonderful visitors from heaven.

Columbus was much impressed with the way the Indians behaved.

"They . . . are so free with all they have, that no one would believe it who has not seen it; of anything that they possess, if it be asked of them, they never say no; on the contrary, they invite you to share it and show as much love as if their hearts went with it."

On October 14th Columbus led his fleet to the far side of the island. There other Indians came to greet them, carrying food and begging the men to come ashore. Some of the sailors went beyond the trees that grew along the sandy beach and saw the Indians' homes, which were small huts shaped like tents around which were gardens where food was raised.

Every day the visitors learned more about these people who lived in harmony and were eager to learn. Columbus, who was careful to treat the Indians kindly, noted their behavior in his journal and in letters to their Royal Majesties.

"They ought to be good servants," he wrote, "and of good skill, for I see that they repeat very quickly all that is said to them; and I believe they could easily be made Christians."

Columbus never considered whether or not the people he found wanted to become Christians, if they had any religion of their own, or if he had a right to enslave them. Like most European Christians in 1492, he believed there was only one God and one true church, the Catholic Church. God had chosen King Ferdinand and Queen Isabella to rule Spain as a Catholic country. When new lands were discovered by Spanish explorers, the lands became part of Spain.

The Spaniards were masters and the natives belonged to Spain, just as much as anything else found in these new lands. The white men, who were so far superior in learning, would naturally know best how the Indians should live, or so Columbus thought. He planned to bring several Indians home with him to show them off, along with the gold and other treasures he expected to find. It would be hundreds of years before people realized that treating fellow human beings like this was hardly fair or Christian.

Columbus and his men accepted the gifts the Indians offered, but they also asked about gold. The Indians only shook their heads. They had no gold. If Columbus wanted gold, he would have to go farther south where there was an island where people wore bands of gold on their arms and ankles. To Columbus that island sounded like Cipangu and he prepared to go there.

Actually, this first island Columbus found was a small island of the Bahamas in the Caribbean Sea. Cipangu or Japan was thousands of miles away. Columbus did not know this, but he did know that unless he returned to Spain with some gold and the promise of even more gold, his Grand Enterprise would not be considered a success and he himself would be a failure.

When Columbus left this first island, which he called San Salvador, he took along several members of this Tainos tribe who offered to come as guides and interpreters. He went from island to island, stopping now and then for a landing. Everywhere he stopped, Columbus planted a cross which was often made from the wood found in the nearby forests. He named and charted each place he discovered, claiming it for Spain. The two largest islands were named Ferdinand and Isabella for their Royal Majesties.

No rivers were found on these first islands so Columbus, who needed fresh water for his men, traded for well water and water the Indians collected from rain. He noted in his journal that it rained often, a little bit every day.

He also noted all the unusual things his men found. On one island the explorers discovered a new kind of bed made of cotton that did not rest on the ground, but hung from the walls of a house and swung in the air. The hammock later became popular in Spain and on ships for sailors.

In late October, Columbus became excited by a new clue to the location of Cipangu and the gold. On October 28th the Admiral sighted the land the Indians called Colba, or Cuba, and sailed up a river. Mountains rose above the mangrove trees that grew along the beaches. But if this was Cipangu, or even China itself, the port should be very busy. Trumpeters from Quinsay, the "City of Heaven," should come down to the ships and greet the voyagers.

There were no boats in the harbor and no trumpets sounded. There were only deserted palm-thatched houses not far from shore.

Disappointed, but not discouraged, Admiral Columbus sailed in and out of rivers, where he found people who showed excitement when he held up golden objects. They pointed inland as if to say gold could be found there where the great chief lived.

Columbus sent out a land expedition to find this chief, hoping his men would find the Great Khan of China himself, to whom the Admiral could turn over the letters written in Latin by their Royal Majesties that identified Columbus as a representative of Spain.

While the exploring party was looking for the great chief, the ships sailed in and out of rivers and sent small groups of sailors ashore to explore Cuba.

Martin Alonso Pinzon's men discovered creole pepper and something that appeared to be cinnamon, both of which could be used as spices and would be valuable for trade in Europe.

When the explorers returned to the ships, the men reported that they had not found the Great Khan, but only another tribal leader who lived in a palm-thatched village. The chief, or cacique, treated them well and offered them food and anything else they wanted, but not gold. Columbus was again disappointed. The explorers told of an unusual sight, though. The Indians here liked to sniff smoking leaves called "tobacos." Many years later "tobacos" became as valuable as gold itself, but these early explorers were barely interested in the leaves.

The Admiral might have stayed to explore Cuba further if he had not heard there was yet another island where gold was easily found. Babeque, the Indians said, was the place where gold could be gathered right on the beaches.

Off the fleet went to the east, searching for Babeque. But after a few days, the wind shifted and Columbus thought his fleet would be in danger if he did not change course. The discovery of Babeque would have to wait until the winds were more favorable.

But Captain Pinzon was anxious to get to Babeque. Perhaps he was tired of taking orders from the Admiral. Some time during the early hours of the morning of November 22nd, the Pinta sailed away from the rest of the fleet.

At first Columbus thought the Pinta was in trouble. He expected Captain Pinzon to bring the ship under control at any moment and come back to the fleet, but the Pinta sailed onward, growing smaller and smaller as the distance between it and the other ships widened. Near sunset the Pinta disappeared from sight. The same suspicion formed in everyone's mind. Whether the winds made the trip dangerous or not, Pinzon was on his way to Babeque to gather gold for himself.

Columbus did not change his opinion that finding the gold wasn't worth the risk of losing his ships. He sailed to another island. On December 12th he placed a cross on Bohio, or Haiti, and named this new land Hispaniola. Here the men discovered a woman wearing gold. The more people the explorers found, the more gold they saw.

Finally, a young chief came aboard the Santa Maria accompanied by 200 of his people. The chief, who was intelligent and proud, was pleased to sit at the table with Columbus where he tasted Spanish food for the first time. As a gift for the Admiral, he produced a belt that was decorated with large pieces of gold. Columbus found the young chief just as generous as all the islanders had been.

"He said that if anything here pleased me, the whole island was mine to command," Columbus wrote in his journal with some surprise.

The way the Indians thought about property amazed him because the Indians owned everything in common. Nothing belonged to any one person. This kind of ownership was very different from the way people owned property in Europe, where private property was prized and men fought over gold and other possessions. When the Spaniards asked for anything, even gold, the Indians were willing to share, to give anything whether the Spaniards gave them gifts or not.

In the center of Hispaniola was a place called Cibao. To Columbus, Cibao sounded very much like Cipangu. When he heard there was much gold in Cibao and that Cibao was ruled by a great chief, he was anxious to visit this place and meet the prince who ruled it and whose name was Guacanagari.

The Admiral waited respectfully for an invitation. He spent his time sailing in and out of harbors, making charts that would be useful to future explorers. The invitation to visit Chief Guacanagari came just before Christmas, and Columbus sailed back to meet him.

The waters were smooth and the wind gentle on Christmas Eve. The Santa Maria and the Nina sailed under a new moon that night. The captains and crews knew the way since they had been here before. They assumed it would be an easy voyage, so the men were not as careful as they usually were. Besides, they had all been celebrating the holiest night of the year and had many Indian visitors the past few days. The men were tired and anxious for rest. Even the Santa Maria's master, Juan de la Cosa, and the pilot decided there was nothing to keep them from going to sleep on such a calm evening. They went off to bed, leaving only a young boy in charge of the ship, a boy whose job it was to turn over the half-hour glass.

"Hold the rudder," the master told him, "and keep an eye out for trouble."

No one expected any trouble, but leaving the boy in charge was the worst mistake the pilot and the master could have made. At midnight, with the Christmas star shining down on the peaceful scene, the Santa Maria ran onto a coral reef. At first the boy did not notice the accident, but when the wooden ship began to creak and groan, he shouted for help.

Every moment that passed caused the ship to be lifted higher and higher onto the reef. All hands were on deck in seconds and the Admiral ordered the ship's master and some of the men to go out in the ship's boat with a line and an anchor to try to free the Santa Maria from the reef.

For the second time that night Juan de la Cosa behaved badly. Afraid that the Santa Maria was about to sink, he and his men rowed out to the Nina to save themselves, instead of trying to save their own ship. Captain Yanez sent the men back to help Columbus, but it was too late. The Santa Maria was hopelessly damaged.

The only thing to do was to remove as much of the cargo as possible and try to save some of the ship's timbers before the Santa Maria sank beneath the tropical waters. Columbus sent a message to Chief Guacanagari for help. The chief sent men in canoes who worked beside the sailors all Christmas Day to salvage what they could from the Santa Maria. The next day the chief himself came aboard the Nina to console Columbus over the loss of his flagship.

"I will give you all I have and more," the chief said, "if that will help."

He offered gold and he offered houses for the men who had no place to stay because the Nina could not hold the crews of both ships.

Columbus, who was grateful, began to think that

the accident might not be such a disaster after all. He had found a powerful friend and the gold he needed. Perhaps the accident was part of God's plan.

Since all the sailors could not sail home in the Nina, Columbus decided to establish a Spanish settlement in the Indies and leave some of the men behind. Facing the reef where the Santa Maria sank was a long beach which Columbus chose as the site of the settlement. He named it Navidad, which was the Spanish word for Christmas.

Hearing the good news that gold was not far away, the seamen were anxious to stay and find it. Columbus chose forty men to build the settlement and he appointed Diego de Harana as their commander.

Now Columbus thought of Martin Alonso Pinzon who might at this moment be on his way back to Spain with the news of the successful journey and with a supply of gold from Babeque. The thought of Pinzon's stealing the honor of reporting to their Royal Majesties infuriated Columbus. Announcing the discovery of the Indies was the Admiral's privilege. If he left for Spain at once, perhaps he could arrive before Pinzon.

Columbus decided he could not take the time to visit Guacanagari's village or see Cibao. He had enough gold on board to show King Ferdinand and Queen Isabella. The important thing was to return to Spain as quickly as possible.

6. *The Dark Voyage Home*

Although Columbus was anxious to begin the voyage home, he stopped several times at the outer islands of the Caribbean. While his men went ashore to collect fresh water and food, including yams, a new food that they said tasted like walnuts, Columbus hopefully scanned the horizon for a sail.

He did not like the idea of crossing the Ocean Sea alone. It was winter now and he knew he would encounter rough weather. To his relief the Nina was out only two days when one of the men spotted the Pinta sailing toward them. Columbus wondered if Pinzon, too, had second thoughts about making the trip alone.

When Pinzon met with Columbus, he treated the Admiral with great courtesy. He told a tale of searching for the fleet ever since the November storm blew the Pinta off course. From island to island Pinzon had gone, hearing of the Admiral's visits, but never finding him. News of the loss of the Santa Maria had reached the Pinta through Indian messengers only days ago. Pinzon said he was sorry he had not been with the fleet to help.

Columbus did not believe much of what Captain Pinzon told him, but he said nothing about his doubts.

No matter what their differences, the two navigators needed each other now. Pinzon confided that he had reached Babeque where he did not find any gold, but on a nearby island he and his men had gathered much of the precious metal to dazzle their Royal Majesties in Spain. Finally Pinzon said he was pleased to be making the journey home with the Admiral.

On the 16th of January the two ships left land behind, sailing north by northeast into the open sea. They looked for the westerly winds Columbus promised would bless the journey home and found them. The men hardly had time to be worried when the brisk westerlies appeared and the ships sailed through the water at a speed of 100 miles a day.

For three weeks the voyage was easy. The men went about their work cheerfully and Columbus took time to begin a long letter which he later sent to his good friend Luis de Santangel, Queen Isabella's advisor. In this letter he proudly described his journey.

"I write to tell you that I crossed in thirty-three days from the Canaries to the Indies," he began.

Everything he said pointed to the success of the Grand Enterprise and promised riches for Spain and everyone who had participated in the expedition. He went on to explain that he had not discovered Japan, but on his second trip he expected to visit China and meet the Great Khan.

The Nina led the fleet into the Sargasso Sea, only this time the men showed no fear. They knew the ships would not become trapped in the weeds. The sailors enjoyed sighting birds and fishing for porpoises, as well as one very large shark. One day they saw a school of tuna.

"Maybe we can show them the way to the tuna factory in Cadiz," Columbus remarked and the men helped themselves to a good laugh.

By February 12th the time for laughter was over. The wind changed abruptly, the skies grew dark and suddenly the sea was so rough that waves rose above the ship and crashed onto the decks of the caravels with frightening force. The Nina began to pitch and roll so violently that the men rushed to lash everything down, holding desperately to lines themselves to avoid being washed overboard.

All that day and into the next night, winds roared and the waves grew into mountains. The men prayed constantly. The Nina and the Pinta tried to stay in contact with each other by signaling with flares which could barely be seen in the fog and rain. On February 14th the Pinta disappeared a second time. No one expected to see her again. The crew of the Nina feared they, too, would be plunged to the bottom of the ocean.

It was the custom in times of terrible danger for sailors to promise to make special journeys or pilgrimages to shrines if the crew survived. The Admiral organized three lotteries. Chick peas were put into a red cap and one pea was marked with a cross. The man who selected the marked pea must represent the crew and make the journey. Twice Columbus himself chose the marked pea. The men thought this was a good sign, but the storm continued.

Finally the men made one more promise. If they survived, they would form a procession, dressed only in their long shirts as a sign of penitence, and visit the first shrine they found that was dedicated to Our Lady.

When the winds did not lessen and the clouds grew darker, Columbus went to his cabin and admitted to himself that he was afraid the ship could not reach Spain. Hastily he wrote a short account of the journey, wrapped it in oil cloth and threw it overboard in a sealed barrel in the hope that someone would learn of his discoveries after the Nina went down.

That very evening the winds subsided and the waves grew smaller. The worst of the storm was over, but where were they now? How far had the winds taken them from their course? Columbus thought they should soon be within sight of one of the Azores, the group of Portuguese Islands west of Spain.

He steered east by northeast and at sunrise on February 15th a seaman sighted the Portuguese island of Santa Maria. The Nina had reached the Azores just as Columbus said she would, but the last thing he wanted to do was make a stop at those islands.

Because Portugal and Spain were such serious rivals in their race to trade with the Indies, he was afraid for the safety of his men and the ship in Portuguese waters, but there was nothing else he could do. The ship needed repairs and the men needed food and water. The Nina sailed into a harbor near a small village, much to the amazement of fishermen who were working nearby. They stared in awe at the Indians who walked the deck of the Nina and they marveled at the tales told by the sailors of their adventures.

From the fishermen the sailors learned of a shrine dedicated to Our Lady. Columbus allowed half the men to leave the ship to fulfill the vow they had made during the terrible storm. Dressed only in their long shirts, their heads bowed, the men walked through the village to hear mass. The sailors had hardly begun to pray when they were arrested and thrown into jail.

Aboard the Nina, Columbus could not imagine what had happened to his crew. The local ruler soon drew alongside the ship in a small boat and announced that he had given the order to arrest the men.

"No one here believes your story of having reached the Indies," he told Columbus scornfully. "What you reached were islands that are part of Africa, islands that belong to Portugal. You are a liar and a braggart."

Enraged by this insult, Columbus threatened to capture a hundred villagers to take back to Spain as slaves if his men were not returned at once. With a scornful flourish he displayed the official letters he carried from their Royal Majesties, which identified him as an official explorer for Spain. The next day Columbus' men were released and the Admiral was invited into the town to be honored by the villagers, but Columbus did not accept the invitation. As soon as he could, he sailed for Palos.

As the ship drew closer to their home port, Columbus wondered where Martin Pinzon was. Had the Pinta survived the terrible storm? Was Pinzon even now reporting to Queen Isabella and King Ferdinand, taking for himself the glory of discovery? The Admiral moved ahead faster.

But there was yet another delay when the Nina sailed into a vicious storm that destroyed all but one of the ship's sails and made Columbus think this was the worst day of the journey. But by daybreak on March 4th, the skies cleared. Giving thanks for this second miraculous escape, Columbus sailed for the nearest port which was Lisbon, Portugal, where he planned to stay just long enough to repair the Nina. News of his arrival spread quickly throughout the city, however, and it wasn't long before King John asked Columbus to visit him. How could he refuse a request from the king?

Columbus walked through the streets of Lisbon, remembering the poor sailor he had once been. He must have seen the Convento dos Santos where he had met his wife Dona Felipa and the shop where he and Bartholomew sold maps and charts. At the royal court he was honored by King John who had once turned down Columbus' request for money to fund his Grand Enterprise. Perhaps King John was sorry for that decision when he learned how successful Columbus had been. It was a proud time for Columbus, but he did not stay long in Portugal.

On March 13th the Nina was ready to sail and Columbus left on the last leg of his journey. The men sighted Cape Vincente and fired a salute. As the Nina's guns roared, Columbus remembered the desperate prayer he had offered seventeen years ago when he clung to the oar that helped him float to shore after his ship had gone down. God had blessed him then and Columbus had lived to discover a world of souls who would be converted for the glory of God and his Catholic Church.

The Nina sailed up the Tinto River into the harbor at Palos, Spain, on March 15, 1493, greeted by shouts and cheers as people recognized the ship and the banners of the expedition. There was no sign of Martin Alonso Pinzon.

Before leaving his ship, Columbus went to his cabin and completed his journal about his voyage ". . . which I hope in Our Lord will be to the greater glory of Christianity, which to some slight extent already has occurred. These are the last words of the Admiral Don Christopher Columbus concerning his First Voyage to the Indies and their discovery."

Later that day, the Pinta arrived, but Columbus never saw Captain Pinzon again. Pinzon had actually been the first to reach Spain at another city. The Pinta, though battered, had survived the storm, and earlier in February Pinzon had sent a message to their Majesties in Barcelona, begging permission to come to them and report the news of the great discovery.

The voyage had been hard and Pinzon was sick, but he wanted more than anything else to beat Columbus home with the good news of the successful voyage. Instead, their Royal Majesties told Pinzon they did not want to hear the report from anyone but Columbus himself.

Pinzon thought there was always the chance that

the Nina had sunk in the storm and Columbus with it. Then the king and queen would have to turn to the surviving captain, Martin Alonso Pinzon, for a report of the journey. All the glory of discovery would fall to him. When Pinzon saw the Nina in the harbor, he was so disappointed that he went directly home where he died a few weeks later.

Columbus' return was glorious. People who doubted him before, cheered him now. He arrived in Seville on Palm Sunday and led a procession over the bridge and into the city. He was followed by ten Indians wearing gold ornaments and carrying parrots whose brilliant green, red and sapphire feathers attracted much attention.

A few days later the Admiral received a letter from their Majesties addressed to "Don Christopher Columbus, their Admiral of the Ocean Sea, Viceroy and Governor of the Islands that he hath discovered in the Indies."

This letter established that Queen Isabella and King Ferdinand were pleased with the results of the Grand Enterprise. When Columbus arrived at court, the royal couple would not allow him to kneel before them. They rose themselves to greet him and asked him to sit beside them, a very special honor.

During those days in Barcelona, where their Royal Majesties were holding court, Christopher Columbus was the most popular man in all Spain. There were feasts and more processions, and in the royal chapel a prayer was chanted in his honor. Columbus had unlocked the secrets of the world by crossing the mysterious Sea of Darkness to unveil what lay on the other side. He had brought honor to Spain, to his sons and to their families for generations to come.

Another man might have thought such achievements were enough for one lifetime, but not Columbus. He had big plans and he could hardly wait to begin a new adventure.

7. *Dreams to Give*

Christopher Columbus had dreams to give. To their Royal Majesties he promised a permanent settlement in the Indies, barrels of gold and other treasures, conversion of the Indians and positive proof that Colba, or Cuba, was really part of the continent of China. To anyone who joined him on this second voyage he offered gold and riches beyond imagination. Thousands of men hurried to accept his offer. Twelve hundred men were chosen.

Like giant white birds, their winged sails spread wide, seventeen ships skimmed over the Ocean Sea, carrying the men ever closer to their heart's desire. On the deck of his flagship, Mariagalante, the Admiral stood proudly beside his youngest brother, Diego, reveling in the joyous journey. He was only sorry that Bartholomew had not returned from Europe in time to join them. This second voyage would not be as lonely as the first for Columbus. To Diego he could confide his most private thoughts, and this time he need not stand alone against fearful men who viewed him with suspicion.

That autumn of 1493, each day was more perfect than the last. With the trade winds blowing briskly behind them, the vessels sped across smooth waters. At sunset the Admiral ordered sails trimmed. Then the ships clustered together, moving more slowly for safety in the dark. But after morning mass, the caravels broke free, caught the winds and raced each other, eager to reach land.

The voyagers were happy and filled with anticipation of the wonders to be seen and the treasures to be won in the Indies. Many of the travelers were Hidalgos, or Spanish gentlemen, seeking their fortunes. But there were also carpenters, stone cutters, handymen and farmers who would be needed to do the work of building a permanent Spanish settlement.

In the hopes of winning thousands of new souls for the church, priests like Fray Bernal Buil, and Fray Ramon Pane were on board. There were also three Franciscans who carried with them a special gift from Queen Isabella, all the material needed for the first Catholic church in the Indies.

Herds of horses were penned up on deck, their neighing an unfamiliar sound in these waters. Below in the holds, the ships carried seeds to begin crops of wheat, melons and cucumbers along with the grapevines and sugar cane that should flourish in the warm climate.

Soon the settlement would be self-sufficient and a regular trade route would be established between Spain and her colony, adding great wealth to the royal treasury. None of this would have been possible if it had not been for the Lord Admiral and Governor, Christopher Columbus, the man who made dreams come true.

The men thought little of the Indians who were

already living on the island of Hispaniola and how they would react to a Spanish settlement there. The Indians were gentle, friendly people, Columbus said, who shared whatever they had, and looked upon the white foreigners as gods. Why wouldn't they share their land with their new Christian neighbors?

The route Columbus followed was a bit south of the one he had taken on the first voyage. On this journey he discovered the shortest distance between the Canary Islands and the Indies. In just three weeks, in the early hours of the morning of November 3rd, the cry of "Tierra! Que Tenemos Tierra! Land! We have land!" rang out from the mast of one of the ships.

A black cone of a volcanic mountain appeared on the horizon as an island of the Lesser Antilles came into view. Columbus named the island Dominica.

But there was no harbor big enough for the fleet at Dominica. Columbus led the way to nearby Guadaloupe where the men gasped in awe at the sight of a waterfall so high in the cloud-covered mountains that it seemed to fall from the sky. Here the ships anchored. Now the men had their first glimpse of terrified Indians, fleeing into the woods at the sight of the tall ships. Who knows what kind of dreadful monsters they imagined on board?

The white men landed and went in search of food, wood and fresh water. But one group of travelers went exploring on its own. When the men did not return in a few hours, search parties marched into the dark woods, sounding trumpets and firing guns.

There was no sign of the men. But in the deserted huts horrible evidence of cannibals, the flesh-eating Caribs, was discovered. Arawak Indians, related to the Tainos Indians Columbus met on his first voyage, were also found. They were being held captive in the huts. The Spaniards brought the gentle Indians to the safety of the ships, and now the search for the missing men became more urgent. What if they had been captured by the man-eating Caribs?

For days Columbus' men roamed the island but could not find the explorers. The Admiral feared the worst. But at sunset on the fourth day the wavering light of a fire was sighted on a hilltop. It was the lost men, signaling for help. Quickly they were rescued and the fleet resumed its journey.

As the ships approached other islands, the Arawaks begged Columbus to frighten the cannibals away and discourage them from going off to capture other peaceful Indians. The Caribs did not frighten easily. Although they had no experience with the powerful cannons and guns the explorers used, the Caribs fought back, often racing out to the ships in dugout canoes to attack the voyagers with spears and crossbows.

Columbus had been told by Queen Isabella to treat the Indians with kindness and love, but now he had to break this rule. He met the Carib attacks with all the force of the weapons he had on board and killed members of the fierce tribe. Now the friendly atmosphere of the first voyage was gone and a feeling of foreboding touched Columbus when he thought of the forty men he had left at the settlement at Navidad. Were they well? Were they safe?

The fleet started for Navidad, but the winds were not favorable and much time was wasted. Finally, on November 27th, the Mariagalante led the ships to a point where they were within sight of the settlement which was ominously dark. No fires flickered in the night and no sound came to the fleet over the quiet waters.

Remembering the hidden reef that had destroyed the Santa Maria in the dark, Columbus dared not sail closer until daylight. Instead, he ordered guns fired and flares set off to notify the men of his presence. The night was suddenly filled with light and sound, but no answering guns roared on the silent island.

No one slept well on board the ships that night. Columbus paced his deck. Now the crew members and passengers who had sailed cheerfully these eight weeks became somber as the dream Columbus had offered them began to fade.

The men were tired and in need of rest. They had expected to find a flourishing settlement of stone houses and a fort at Navidad where barrels of gold should already have been stored away, ready and waiting to be shipped home to Spain. If this part of the dream was not true, then what other disappointments awaited everyone?

In the light of morning the reality was horribly clear. There was no settlement. Navidad had been burned to the ground and every one of the forty men had been killed. From the friendly Tainos Indians and Chief Guacanagari himself the facts were pieced together. The men Columbus had left behind had not tried to farm. They lived by taking what they needed from their Indian neighbors. When the settlers abused their new friends by ordering the Indians to find gold for them, an angry tribe led by Chief Caonabo rose against the Spaniards in a terrible fury.

Chief Guacanagari told all he knew while lying in his hammock where he said he was recovering from a wound he had gotten in the battle. He said he had tried to help the settlers because he thought his friend the Admiral would expect that of him.

Many of the men with Columbus did not believe Chief Guacanagari's story. They thought he, too, was guilty of slaughtering the settlers and they urged Columbus to put the chief to death. Columbus refused to allow anyone to harm his friend. There was no proof, he said, that Guacanagari was guilty of treachery.

This did not change the fact that there were now unfriendly tribes on Hispaniola under Chief Caonabo. Somewhere deep in the mountains was the gold mine of Cibao. It would not be easy to get to the mine with enemies lurking in the forest. How different these Indians and the Caribs were from the reports Columbus had given of Indians who were all so friendly and timid that "fifty would not take on one Spaniard"!

Many of the men thought Columbus had deliberately lied to their Royal Majesties and everyone else. The Indies was not the wonderful place he described. The dream of the comfortable life in the islands where treasure was easily collected and men became rich overnight faded further.

Columbus had a group of hostile men on his hands who were not as ready to be disciplined on land as they had been at sea. As Governor, he determined to begin again by abandoning the site of the failed settlement.

With Diego Alvarez Chanca, the ship's doctor, Columbus found a healthier, more pleasant place to settle, a wooded peninsula. He named the place Isabela and planned to build a walled city here with a stone fort, a plaza, a governor's palace for himself and sturdy houses for the men. While the work was getting started in January, he sent Alonso de Hojeda and Gines de Gorbalan, two strong leaders, with thirty men and Indian guides to find the gold of Cibao. Gold would raise everyone's spirits.

Before the end of the month, the men returned with large valuable golden nuggets, as well as other gifts of gold from friendly Indians the men had encountered. Delighted with the discovery, Columbus was anxious to send the men back to find the actual mine. But by late January the new settlement was in trouble.

Three or four hundred men were sick, for the tropical climate and the food did not agree with them. Others were recovering from illnesses and unable to work. Those who could work, refused, insisting that they were gentlemen and had not come to work with their hands.

Columbus realized he would have to send the sick and disillusioned travelers back to Spain. Twelve ships, commanded by Antonio de Torres, would carry them home. Columbus also sent letters to their Royal Majesties and to friends at court, hoping to counteract the bad impression these men would give of his second expedition.

Columbus sent no complaints. He described the fast, easy voyage and the samples of gold he had already collected. He asked for supplies, shoes, weapons and experienced miners to work the gold mine. He asked that three or four caravels be sent back immediately "with salt meat and wheat, wine, oil and vinegar, sugar and molasses, as well as medicine for the sick and almonds, raisins, honey and rice" for those who were getting well.

Debating whether or not to send back the large golden nuggets which had been discovered, Columbus decided to wait until his men had enough gold to send home in barrels. Only large amounts of gold would impress their Majesties and the critics who were sure to speak out against him. Instead, Columbus sent back a number of Caribs to be sold as slaves, even though he knew Queen Isabella would not approve. At least the Caribs would bring in money.

But Columbus knew that only gold would make the difference between success and failure. The gold mine must be found without delay.

8. The Haunted Settlement

In March of 1494, a fearsome sight met the Indians of Hispaniola. Men on horseback thundered through the mountains. Never having seen horses before, the Indians were terrified by the large animals and even wondered if the riders were all part of the same dreadful beasts. What the Indians were witnessing was an expedition led by Columbus to the gold mine of Cibao. The explorers traveled to the sound of trumpets that shattered the stillness of the forests and sent timid birds soaring from their nests.

After the Indians overcame their fear of the horses, they welcomed the men into their villages, sharing whatever they had with the visitors. Deep in the mountains, Columbus chose a place for a fort which he expected his men to build to protect the gold mine which must be nearby. Hadn't the explorers found gold dust in the streams and nuggets buried in the soil along the way? There had to be a gold mine in Cibao.

Columbus knew he could not spend all his time exploring. He was Governor of Hispaniola and had to tend to his duties at the settlement where his brother Diego was temporarily in charge. Leaving a group of

men to begin the building of the fort under Mosen Pedro Margarit, Columbus returned to Isabela and found a group of angry men. Diego was not a good leader. He was unable to get the hidalgos to do the work of carpenters when the workers fell ill. Diego kept some kind of order by severely punishing those who disobeyed him, which only made the men more angry.

Determined to make a success of the settlement, Columbus sent Alonso de Hojeda with a number of the troublesome men into the mountain to relieve Margarit and protect the fort against an attack from Chief Caonabo. Instead of ordering Margarit and his men home, Columbus directed them to form an exploring party to roam the island, looking for treasure and living off the land. This would keep some of the discontented men away from Isabela for a while so the loyal hard-working settlers could build the city in peace.

Columbus then made the mistake of leaving Diego again in charge of the settlement while he went about the business of the expedition. He had promised their Royal Majesties that he would find proof that Colba or Cuba was really a part of the continent of China.

The Portuguese insisted that Columbus had not reached the Orient and had only discovered islands that really belonged to Portugal because the Portuguese had been exploring islands of the Ocean Sea for years. The king of Portugal was so sure he was right that he appealed to the pope to consider the problem of how to divide the lands in the Ocean Sea between

Spain and Portugal by drawing an imaginary line of demarcation in the ocean. Those lands found west of the line would belong to Spain. Those lands found east of the line would belong to Portugal. Proof that Columbus had found China would weigh heavily in Spain's favor and convince the pope to place the line in such a position that Spain could keep and settle the islands Columbus had already discovered as well as any other lands he might find.

Taking the remaining five ships, and using the Nina for himself as flagship, Columbus reached Cuba in five days. The land of southern Cuba was not as attractive as the northern coast which he had visited on his first voyage. Mountains rose in steep steps above the sea so the land was hard to approach. It did not look as fertile or as green as the northern lands. At the end of the first day of exploration along the southern coast, the ships sailed into a large, deserted harbor which today is called Guantanamo Bay where the United States maintains a naval base. Columbus called the bay Puerto Grande.

His passengers were not impressed. If Cuba were part of China, where was the evidence of the advanced Chinese civilization? Where were the busy harbors filled with the Chinese boats that Marco Polo described so vividly? Where were the cities and the Chinese people?

When Columbus learned from some Indians that there was gold in nearby Jamaica, he went there at once, hoping to soothe the grumbling men with treasure. What the fleet found was a magnificent island, brilliantly green above a deep blue sea.

"It is the fairest island that eyes have beheld:

mountainous and the land seems to touch the sky . . ." Columbus said.

But there was no gold and Columbus sailed back to Cuba to continue his exploration of the southern coast. Late in May of 1494, the ships ran into trouble. They sailed into waters that mysteriously changed color from milk white, to deep blue, to green and then black. The waters actually took on the color of minerals at the bottom of the sea, but the superstitious men did not know this. They were frightened and thought the changing colors were a bad sign. They clamored to go back to Hispaniola, but Columbus was a stubborn man. He did not understand the changing colors any better than anyone else, but he wanted to prove that he had reached China. He became unreasonable and would not turn back, even if it meant putting his passengers and crew in danger.

The fleet ran into one difficulty after another. The ships were damaged time and time again by running aground in shallow water. They were soon leaking badly. By June the men were sick as well as disappointed, and everyone was afraid the weakened ships would never get them back to Isabela.

Columbus tried to ignore the pleas to return, but these men were not the simple seamen he had commanded on his first voyage. They were gentlemen of Spain. Columbus could not force his will on them, but he hated to fail. If he went back now, their Royal Majesties would want to know why he had not completed his mission.

Finally Columbus resorted to a desperate measure. He called the chief scribe, Perez de Luna, to him and said, "Ask each man to sign an oath saying he believes this land is the continent of China and not an island. Then we will turn back."

Among the penalties for breaking such an oath was having your tongue cut out. Columbus was confident that no one aboard would find it easy to deny the oath later. He also knew that such an oath proved nothing, but the oaths from every gentlemen aboard would suggest that further exploration of the island was not necessary at the time and Columbus was right to return to Isabela without completing his mission. Every man signed the oath, and on June 13th the small fleet turned around and started back to Isabela.

The trip was not easy because the winds were against them. Rough waters and dangerous coral reefs rose up to threaten the weakened ships. It took 25 days to go 200 miles. On Sunday, July 7th, the winds were calm and the Admiral went ashore to hear mass.

During the ceremony a dignified old Indian observed what the men were doing. Afterwards he came to speak to Columbus, offering him fruit and sitting beside him on the beach. Through an interpreter he talked to the Lord Admiral and described the similarities he saw in the way the Indians and the white men understood religion.

"I wanted to tell you that we believe in the life hereafter. Departing souls go in two directions: one is bad, full of darkness, where those who do evil to men go; the other is good and happy, and peace-loving people go there. Therefore, if you feel you must die and believe that every man answers for his deeds after death, you will not harm those who do not harm you."

He added that the mass seemed good to him because he could see that the men were giving thanks
to God.

Columbus was surprised at the old Indian's un-
derstanding of God's world. He explained that he believed in heaven and hell, too, and that he had been
sent by his king and queen to gather information
about the islands and to protect the Indians who were
being harmed by the Caribs.

The old Indian was pleased to hear this and so
impressed with Columbus that he said if it had not
been for his wife and children, he would beg to go
back to Spain with Columbus to meet this holy king
and queen.

The rest of the journey was no easier than the
first part. Columbus walked the deck of the Nina day
and night, intent on getting his passengers safely to
port. He had very little sleep and he thought constantly of his disappointment at not finding the Great
Khan and proof that Cuba was China.

The strain was too much for him and just before
the ships reached Isabela, the Admiral fell ill with a
fever. In late September he was carried ashore at Isabela where the settlers were at war with the Indians
as well as one another.

Margarit, who led the band of men Columbus had
told to make explorations and live off the land, spent
his time looking for gold and forcing Indians to feed
his men. When Diego ordered him to follow the
queen's order to treat the Indians well, Margarit
stormed into Isabela, seized three caravels, and sailed

back to Spain with Fray Buil and other angry men who would certainly speak against Columbus to their Royal Majesties.

Fortunately, the news was not all bad in Isabela. While Columbus was gone, four ships arrived from Spain with needed supplies. On one of these ships was Bartholomew Columbus, who was carrying a letter for his brother from their Royal Majesties, a glowing letter of support and praise for the Admiral.

"Their Highnesses . . . regard as a very signal service of the Admiral all that he has done and is doing, for they appreciate that next to God it is to him that they are indebted for all they had and will have herein. . . ."

Even this high praise could not cheer Columbus, but Bartholomew did. With his help Columbus regained his health. When he was well enough, Columbus redoubled his efforts to find gold. He stayed in the Indies for another year and a half, trying unsuccessfully to keep order in the new settlement and among the Indians who had turned against the Spaniards.

Thousands of Indians were killed as Columbus and the explorers grew more anxious for treasure. Columbus would have done well to remember his conversation with the old Indian in Cuba. Perhaps he did remember, but his desire to make his original dream of finding wealth for Spain in the Indies come true overcame his sense of right and wrong. He no longer concerned himself with building the settlement at Isabela. The work was all but abandoned in favor of looking for gold.

Finally this second settlement was abandoned,

too, because it became clear there was no gold in Cibao and the Indians who fought so valiantly to save themselves from the cruelties of the Spaniards had nearly all been killed. The many people who lost their lives in Isabela seemed to haunt the place and few men ever returned to visit.

One man who did visit told of a ghostly experience. He was walking along the square in the deserted settlement when he suddenly came upon a group of well-dressed Spanish gentlemen. Surprised to see anyone in this dismal place, he greeted the hidalgos who solemnly bowed and raised their hands to remove their hats. But when they did, their heads came off as well and suddenly the men's bodies crumbled into dust like the dreams of wealth, glory and peace with newly Christianized Indians who died in Isabela.

9. A Dream Fades

Columbus arrived in Spain in June of 1496. No crowds were waiting to greet him. He did not expect them. He knew his name no longer held the magic it had three years earlier. Many people thought Columbus was a failure. Where was all the gold he had bragged about? Why had he not found the Great Khan and visited China?

Just before Columbus left Hispaniola, Juan Aguado, an investigator sent by their Royal Majesties, arrived with orders to look into the rumors about Columbus' poor leadership. Aguado also carried a royal letter, ordering Columbus to distribute new supplies fairly because men complained he had not been fair with supplies in the past.

Hurt that their Royal Majesties would think he had been dishonest, Columbus knew it was time to go home and defend himself. It was true that he had not distributed supplies equally to the men who refused to work, but this was the only way he could maintain some kind of order. It was also true he had not completed his mission satisfactorily. Columbus took responsibility for his failures, but he hoped the king and queen would understand the difficulties he had faced and give him another chance.

Confident and strong after a brief rest, the Admiral presented his report, explaining his own disappointment at not achieving all that had been expected of him. He was happy to learn that the king and queen were still grateful to him for leading the way to the Indies and that they were willing to give him six ships for his third voyage.

Three of the ships would go to Hispaniola at once with needed supplies, while Columbus used the other three for a special mission. He was to search for a continent the king of Portugal insisted lay south of the islands Columbus had already discovered and to the east of the pope's line of demarcation. If such a continent was found west of the line instead, Spain, not Portugal, would have the right to great riches in this new land and could claim the mission to baptize the people living there.

The Admiral was also ordered to chart and claim for Spain all lands lying south of the islands he had already discovered, because it was believed that lands in southern latitudes contained more valuable products like gold, gems and spices, which the Portuguese had found in Africa.

Enthusiastic as he was about this trip, Columbus was skeptical about the existence of a continent south of Cuba, which he assumed was China, but he believed firmly in the importance of his finding lands with valuable products that would keep Spain interested in the Indies.

Two years later the Admiral was preparing for this third voyage. It was difficult to find men who wanted to accompany him after news of the cruel life in the Indies and the lack of plentiful gold had spread through Spain. Finally it was decided that any prisoners who would give two years' work in the Indies could win their freedom. There were plenty of men in prison who were anxious to be free. They agreed to join Columbus. This time some women signed aboard as well. Soon there would be Spanish families living in Santo Domingo.

The journey started on May 30, 1498. Four weeks later Columbus reached Trinidad, a small island off the coast of the very continent he had been sent to find.

Trinidad was so beautiful that he wrote in his journal, "These lands are so fair and so verdant and full of trees and palms that they are superior to the gardens of Valencia in May."

Sailing west, the Admiral reached a peninsula on the northern coast of South America which he called Paria. At first Columbus thought he had discovered another island. But after seeing the fresh water that flowed from the rivers into the sea and realizing the depth of the gulf through which he had passed, he wrote: "I believe that this is a very great continent, which until today has been unknown."

Though Columbus admitted the possibility of a continent, he never stopped believing he had found the Indies, rather than an entirely new world. He thought this new continent was a land south of China, a land Marco Polo had missed as he sailed the Indian Ocean to visit the Great Khan.

Perhaps if Columbus had been able to give up his belief that he had discovered the Indies on the other side of the Ocean Sea, he would have made more of this new continent. Instead, he hurried on to Hispaniola where he hoped to learn his brothers had been able to build an orderly settlement. Before Columbus left Isabela after his second voyage, he and Bartholomew agreed upon a new site for the settlement at a place they called Santo Domingo in honor of their father, Domenico Columbus.

But there was no peace or satisfaction for the Admiral in the new capital. His brothers had managed to build a splendid stone governor's palace, but Columbus found he could not rest there. Rebels led by Francisco Roldan were fighting with Bartholomew and Diego for power. As the months went by, the situation went from bad to worse. There were constant battles among the men and between the Indians and the Spaniards. And though Columbus made many trips into the mountains, he was unable to find the large amounts of gold he needed to send home to Spain.

Columbus lost more of his popularity when Alonso de Hojeda crossed the Ocean Sea to visit and chart Paria, which he realized at once was a large and rich continent. On board Hojeda's ship was a man from Florence, Italy, named Amerigo Vespucci, who later published the story of this voyage. Soon people were calling the New World "America" after this man who had little more to do with its discovery than write about it.

Another explorer, Peralonso Nino, who had sailed with Columbus on his first voyage, got permission to sail across the Ocean Sea, too. He followed the South American coast and found the mouth of the Amazon River. Part of the land he discovered in

South America was divided by the Line of Demarcation. That land to the east of the line belonged to Portugal, which soon began to colonize it. Eventually Brazil became the only Portuguese-speaking country in South America. The larger part of the continent, because of its position west of the Line of Demarcation, belonged to Spain.

The king and queen of Spain were most pleased by Nino's discovery, which was the very thing they had hoped Columbus would do for them. Now, too, their scholars were saying that Columbus' view of the world was wrong, that he had *not* discovered the Indies which must lie far beyond the newly-found continent. It seemed the world was much larger than anyone had suspected. Columbus, they said, was too stubborn to admit the truth.

Queen Isabella, who had always supported Columbus, was growing annoyed with him for sending home Indian slaves when she had made it very clear that she did not want him to do this. Besides everything else, there was so much trouble among the settlers in Santo Domingo that their Royal Majesties appointed Francisco de Bobadilla to investigate the situation.

When Bobadilla sailed into the harbor at Santo Domingo, the first thing he saw were the bodies of rebels hanging in the square. More men were to be executed shortly. Because Columbus and his brother Bartholomew were away fighting an uprising outside the city, Diego had to face the Chief Justice Bobadilla alone.

"Release the imprisoned men to me until I can investigate the charges against them," Bobadilla ordered.

Diego refused and Bobadilla promptly put Diego in prison. It wasn't long before Christopher Columbus and Bartholomew found themselves in chains, too. All three brothers were shipped back to Spain in disgrace. A proud man, Columbus refused to have his chains removed until he reached Spain and their Royal Majesties ordered his release themselves.

When the king and queen heard how badly Columbus had been treated, they sent for him at once. They made sure he received all his back income, which was ten percent of all the trading done with the Indies. But they did not reinstate him as Governor of the Indies, nor did they recall Bobadilla as Columbus asked.

The king and queen assured their Admiral that they were still pleased with him and grateful for the important work he had done for Spain. Relieved that his reputation had not been completely destroyed by his enemies, Christopher Columbus begged for one last voyage. If he was allowed to make a fourth voyage, he said he would search for the Passage to India, a water route between China and the southern continent, that would prove once and for all that he had discovered the Indies and all those who said he had not were wrong.

Finally their Royal Majesties agreed that Columbus deserved this chance. The High Voyage, as Columbus called his fourth voyage, began on April 3, 1502. But the expedition was not a success. The Passage to India was never found, and Columbus returned to Spain two years later in November of 1504, weakened by his adventures and in poor health, only to have King Ferdinand and Queen Isabella ignore him and his request to be reinstated as Governor of the Indies. For Columbus his dream had all but faded.

10. The Man Who Unlocked the Secrets of the World

Fresh spring air drifted through the windows of a small brick house in Valladolid, Spain. Bells sounded in the church of the nearby monastery, calling the friars to morning prayers and briefly rousing Christopher Columbus from a troubled sleep.

Crippled with arthritis and plagued by other illnesses, the Admiral was weak and near death. Few people admired him or even remembered him any more. Queen Isabella had died and King Ferdinand seldom contacted him, though Columbus repeatedly wrote to him, insisting that the king honor the agreement they had made before the first voyage, promising to Columbus the titles and honors of Governor of the Indies and Admiral of the Ocean Sea for himself and for his sons for all time.

The trouble, Columbus knew, began in Isabela on his second voyage and it haunted him as it haunted the ruins in Hispaniola. Too many Spaniards and Indians had died at Isabela. The echo of the tragedies touched every part of the New World. For the cruelty to the Indians that began in Isabela grew as time went by. The men who arrived in their tall ships and who had once been received as friends, as "men from Heaven," in 1492, repaid the gentle Indians with greed and cruelty that changed their civilization forever.

What had become of Columbus' dream to be a Christ Bearer? Why had he betrayed and enslaved the Indians?

Much of his behavior was prompted by his desire to bring about law and order, as well as his need to send home the treasure he had promised his king and queen. In both endeavors he had failed. But there was one achievement of which he could be proud, although even Columbus nearly lost sight of it at the end of his life.

On his last voyage Columbus believed God revealed the truth to him in a dream. At the time the Admiral was under attack by Indians off the coast of Panama. Alone and ill, Columbus thought he would lose his ship and die without ever returning to Spain. He cried out for help and he prayed. Then he fell into a deep sleep and a comforting voice came to him.

". . . O fool and slow to believe and serve thy God, the God of every man! What more did He do for Moses or for David His servant than for thee? . . . Of those barriers of the Ocean Sea, which were closed with such mighty chains, He gave thee the keys."

On May 20, 1506, in his rented house in Valladolid, Columbus hardly recognized the difference between waking and sleeping, or noticed the family and friends who came to be with him. He was dying, an unhappy old man who thought he had been forgotten by the very people who once cheered and admired him. But perhaps before he died that same comforting voice came to him again and repeated its message:

"Of those barriers of the Ocean Sea, which were closed with such mighty chains, He gave thee the keys."

Columbus dared to sail where no one had sailed before. With great faith in God and God's plan for him, he took "the keys" and unlocked the secrets of the world. For that achievement the world admires Christopher Columbus and always will.

Bibliography

Cohen, J. M., Editor. *The Four Voyages of Christopher Columbus.* Baltimore: Penguin Books, 1969.

Floyd, Troy S. *The Columbus Dynasty in the Caribbean 1492–1526.* Albuquerque: University of New Mexico Press, 1973.

Granzotto, Gianni. *Christopher Columbus, The Dream and the Obsession.* Garden City: Doubleday & Company, Inc., 1985.

Irving, Washington. *The Voyages of Columbus.* Halbert, Winifred, Editor. New York: Frederick Ungar Publishing Co., 1960.

Keen, Benjamin, translator. *The Life of the Admiral Christopher Columbus by His Son Ferdinand.* New Brunswick: Rutgers University Press, 1959.

Las Casas, Bartolome de. Collard, Andree, translator and editor. *History of the Indies.* New York: Harper & Row, 1971.

87

Meltzer, Milton. *Columbus and the World Around Him*. New York: Franklin Watts, 1990.

Morison, Samuel Eliot. *Admiral of the Ocean Sea: A Life of Christopher Columbus*. Boston: Little, Brown and Company, 1942.

———. *Christopher Columbus, Mariner*. Boston: Little, Brown and Company, 1955.

Morison, Samuel Eliot and Obregon, Mauricio. *The Caribbean As Columbus Saw It*. Boston: Atlantic Monthly Press, 1964.

Sales, Kirkpatrick. *The Conquest of Paradise*. New York: Alfred A. Knopf, 1990.

Sanderlin, George. *Across the Ocean Sea, A Journal of Columbus's Voyage*. New York: Harper & Row, 1966.